# MR. SELFRIDGE'S

## ROMANCE

### of

## COMMERCE

*An* ABRIDGED VERSION *of the* CLASSIC TEXT *on*
**BUSINESS AND LIFE**

*Harry Gordon Selfridge*

▲adamsmedia
AVON, MASSACHUSETTS

Contains material adapted and abridged from *The Romance of Commerce* by Harry Gordon
Selfridge, copyright © 1918 by John Lane Company.

Published by
Adams Media, a division of F+W Media, Inc.
57 Littlefield Street, Avon, MA 02322. U.S.A.
*www.adamsmedia.com*

ISBN 10: 1-4405-6909-6
ISBN 13: 978-1-4405-6909-8
eISBN 10: 1-4405-6910-X
eISBN 13: 978-1-4405-6910-4

Printed in the United States of America.

10 9 8 7 6 5 4 3 2 1

**Library of Congress Cataloging-in-Publication Data**

Selfridge, H. Gordon (Harry Gordon), 1856-1947.
    [Romance of commerce]
    Mr. Selfridge's Romance of commerce : an abridged version of the classic text on business
and life / Harry Gordon Selfridge.
        pages cm
    Includes bibliographical references and index.
    ISBN-13: 978-1-4405-6909-8 (hard cover : alk. paper)
    ISBN-10: 1-4405-6909-6 (hard cover : alk. paper)
    ISBN-13: 978-1-4405-6910-4 (electronic)
    ISBN-10: 1-4405-6910-X (electronic)
1. Commerce--History. 2. Great Britain--Commerce--History. I. Title. II. Title: Mister
Selfridge's Romance of commerce.
    HF352.S453 2013
    381.09--dc23

2013018095

Cover and interior images © iStockphoto.com/aleksandarvelasevic,
iStockphoto.com/DavidGoh, 123RF.com, and clipart.com.

*This book is available at quantity discounts for bulk purchases.
For information, please call 1-800-289-0963.*

# INTRODUCTION

*B*oth to contemporaries and to us at the distance of nearly a century, Harry Gordon Selfridge seems bigger than reality. In the course of a life that began and ended in genteel poverty, he rose to become one of the most famous men in Europe. He transformed the department store, changed advertising forever, and embarked on a series of glittering love affairs with some of the great beauties of his age. When we enter a department store today and find ourselves facing the perfume and makeup counters on the first floor, we are seeing the work of Harry Selfridge. When we stop to admire striking widow displays that draw crowds during the holiday season, we are paying tribute to the genius of Harry Selfridge.

Selfridge might almost have inspired the young-man-born-into-poverty-and-makes-good novels of Horatio Alger. Fighting his way up the economic and social ladder, he started delivering newspapers when he was ten years old in order to supplement the family income. Before he was twenty-one, he was working for the famed Chicago store owner Marshall Field. There he coined the classic advertising line "Only _____ shopping days until Christmas" and possibly originated the phrase (much hated by sales clerks) "The customer is always right." He also found time to marry the beautiful Chicago heiress and property developer Rose Buckingham.

It was a time of rapid change. In 1893, the Chicago World's Fair drew millions of visitors to the city's south side, where they rode the world's first Ferris wheel and strolled among the buildings of the White City built along the Midway (the inspiration for L. Frank Baum's Emerald City of Oz). Walking among the people, Selfridge noted what it took to entertain and excite a large crowd—thoughts that would later bear rich fruit.

Fashion, like everything else, was in flux. The large, stiff dresses of the later Victorian period were giving way to softer, more practical clothing. Princess Alexandra, the Prince of Wales's wife, made popular the "two-piece." By the turn of the century, the bustle had largely disappeared; women wore high-necked blouses, swept their hair up, and took advantage of the new freedom their clothing allowed them. Among those who did so was the dancer Isadora Duncan, who became a friend (some said lover) of Harry Selfridge.

All these new fashions were on display at Marshall Field's, but Selfridge wanted more—he wanted his *own* store, where he could put into practice his theories about advertising and display.

In 1906, while on a trip to London, he determined to expand into the Old World. He left Field's and on March 15, 1909, opened Selfridges at the west end of Oxford Street. The opening was somewhat less than ideal: it rained heavily, and inside the store the crush of visitors overtaxed the bathrooms and drinking fountains, causing a water shortage (the manager of the hairdressing salon, so the story goes, ran to the restaurant and grabbed siphons of soda water to rinse out shampoos from his customers' hair). Nonetheless, the store was an immediate hit, with more than a million visitors during its first week.

In retrospect it isn't hard to see why. Selfridges was, simply, a different kind of department store. Massive amounts of space were given over to "services," including a library, a restaurant, the aforementioned hair salon, and a smoking room. Selfridge believed that you got people into the store and then kept them there. Later, Selfridges was marked by massive displays—everything from a monoplane used in the first cross-Channel flight—to a seismograph. The first public demonstration of television was made in 1925 in Selfridges.

Selfridge himself, flushed with commercial success, continued to expand his repertoire of lovers, including the dancer Anna Pavlova, the writer Elinor Glyn (whose sister was a leading fashion designer of the day), the designer Syrie Maugham (married to writer W. Somerset Maugham), and—spectacularly—the French *chanteuse* Gaby Deslys, whose former lovers had included Prince Wilhelm of Germany, King Manuel of Portugal, and Frank Gould, son of the American robber baron Jay Gould. She posed for society photographs wearing enormous hats, which were then in fashion and sold at Selfridges.

There is no question that these affairs caused tensions in his marriage with Rosalie, with whom, by this time, he had three daughters and a son. However, she suffered in silence, and Harry was genuinely attached to her, making it all the more tragic when she died unexpectedly in 1918. Her death left her husband distraught, and he plunged into work as a palliative. He planned expansions of the store and one as well for his home in Highcliffe Castle near the Isle of Wight. Perhaps fortunately for the surrounding countryside, the latter was never built.

His string of love affairs continued. In Jenny and Rosie Dolly, he found two young women who shared his growing addiction to gambling. This obsession with poker became increasingly problematic after 1929, when the world moved into an economic depression and Selfridges, in common with many businesses, suffered a sharp downturn in sales.

Selfridge had always been free with his spending. Although he and his family were only renters at Highcliffe, he spent more than $3.5 million in today's money renovating and modernizing the castle to suit his tastes. As Britain shuddered through the 1930s, he found his money growing tighter. Even then, though, he was full of new ideas for the store; in 1939 he opened the first television department, convinced the new technology was the future.

However, many within the store's hierarchy—including Selfridge's son, Gordon Jr., who sat on the board—were convinced that the time had come for the aging magnate to make way for younger blood. On October 18, 1939, Selfridge was confronted at a board meeting by a rebellious staff. They pointed out that he owed the store more than £118,000 as well as a quarter-million pounds in back taxes. The situation was no longer tenable, and Selfridge was presented with a letter of resignation for him to sign.

In forced retirement, he slipped gradually into obscurity, dying in 1947. But the store he built, the store that embodied all his hopes, dreams, and innovation, remains. Today, as busy shoppers file along its counters and contemplate their purchases, they are looking at the living legacy of an entrepreneurial genius: Harry Gordon Selfridge.

WE ARE ALL MERCHANTS,

AND ALL RACES OF MEN

HAVE BEEN MERCHANTS IN

SOME FORM OR ANOTHER.

*Commerce, that mother of riches and power, which is always ready to give a share of them to the merchant who comes to her with determination, with sound principles, with judgment and courage.*

TO THE TRUE MERCHANT

OBSTACLES EXIST ONLY

TO BE OVERCOME.

The victories of the modern playing field fade into insignificance before the indomitable pluck and the staying power necessary for ventures where the risk was a man's entire capital, and often his life as well, and the reward, not a silver cup or shield, but a fortune perhaps doubled, and the reputation of an explorer. ঌ

# MONEY!
# WHAT AN
# ENORMOUS
# POWER!

THE ARTIST SELLS THE WORK OF HIS BRUSH AND IN THIS HE IS A MERCHANT. THE WRITER SELLS TO ANY WHO WILL BUY, LET HIS IDEAS BE WHAT THEY WILL. THE TEACHER SELLS HIS KNOWLEDGE OF BOOKS—OFTEN IN TOO LOW A MARKET—TO THOSE WHO WOULD HAVE THIS KNOWLEDGE PASSED ON TO THE YOUNG.

The doctor must make an income to support himself and his family. He too is a merchant. His stock-in-trade is his intimate knowledge of the physical man and his skill to prevent or remove disabilities. He sells a part of his experience for a given sum to whomsoever seeks his advice. The lawyer sometimes knows the laws of the land and sometimes does not, but he sells his legal language, often accompanied by common sense, to the multitude who have not yet learned that a contentious nature may squander quite as successfully as the spendthrift. The statesman sells his knowledge of men and affairs, and the spoken or written exposition of his principles of Government; and he receives in return the satisfaction of doing what he can for his nation, and occasionally wins as well a niche in its temple of fame. 🙚

THE PREACHER, THE LECTURER,
THE ACTOR, THE ESTATE AGENT,
THE FARMER, THE EMPLOYEE, ALL,
ALL ARE MERCHANTS, ALL HAVE
SOMETHING TO DISPOSE OF AT
A PROFIT TO THEMSELVES, AND
THE DIGNITY OF THE BUSINESS
IS DECIDED BY THE MANNER IN
WHICH THEY CONDUCT THE SALE.

To work is elevating. To accomplish is superb. To fill one's time with profitable enterprise is to leap forward in the world's race and to place beside one's name the credit mark of effort. It has always been so since civilization began, and all effort has always had for its object a gain of some kind, while the amount of effort is usually determined by the value of the hoped-for gain, plus the temperament, ambitions, and inclinations of the doer. 〰️

Food, clothing, and shelter, these, in

some degree, must be possessed by every

individual. And the steps from these crudest

beginnings of trade up to the science of

Commerce of the twentieth century are

as interesting to study as the pages of the

wildest romance. ✑

**WEALTH WITH ITS** accompanying power has been since earliest time the goal that no honest effort can be too great to reach; and the goal it must always remain for peoples who have the red blood of progress in their veins. And without Commerce there is no wealth. ⚘

*While the soil so amply repays labor expended upon it, the owner of the crops looks to the alchemist, Commerce, to turn his golden harvests into golden coin.*

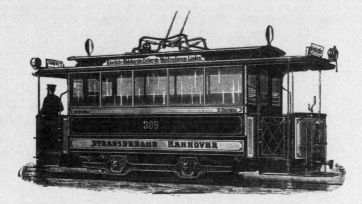

If Commerce is necessary to wealth, no Commerce means no wealth, and our statesman soon finds himself out of employment. Where wealth again is greatest, everything else being fairly equal, arts thrive the most.

COMMERCE CREATES WEALTH,
AND IS THE FOUNDATION OF
THE GREAT STATE. ARMIES ARE
RAISED AND PAID FOR TO WIN,
OR TO PROTECT THE COUNTRIES'
TRADE, OR COMMERCE. SHIPS
ARE CONSTRUCTED, COLONIES
ESTABLISHED, INVENTIONS
ENCOURAGED, GOVERNMENTS
BUILT UP, OR PULLED DOWN,
FOR COMMERCE.

**P**eople must be governed, and there must be those who govern. Laws must be made, and there must be those who study, and those who execute, these laws. People must be taught, and there must be teachers. All these and the Church, the newspaper, the theatre, the fine arts are essential to the completeness of the State, to the happiness and safety of its people; but Commerce is the main stem, or trunk, where they are all branches, supplied with the sap of its far-reaching wealth. ❧

The desire to trade seems to be inherent in man, as natural to him as the instinct of self-preservation, and from earliest recorded history we see trade and barter entering into and becoming part of the lives of men of all nations, and further, we see it as one of the most desirable objectives of the nations themselves.

THAT COUNTRY IN WHICH TRADE

FLOURISHES IS ACCOUNTED

HAPPY, WHILE THAT IN WHICH

COMMERCE DROOPS PROVOKES

SHAKING OF HEADS AND

PROPHECIES OF DOWNFALL.

Just as in a beautiful tapestry there must be the groundwork, the foundation upon which the design is woven, so has commerce acted as the underlying warp and woof in the development of civilization. It gives both strength and substance, and more than this, for it gives color as well. Its threads are so closely interwoven with the rest as to be almost indistinguishable from them.

Commerce is the mother of the arts, the sciences, the professions, and in this twentieth century has itself become an art, a science, a profession. As it plays with a fine touch on the strings of human nature the world over, and makes happier by its fairness the youth of today and the man of tomorrow, it is an art.

Commerce is the foundation upon
which nations are built; but it is also
the superstructure, and provides the
bands of steel which support every
part of the national edifice.

**E**ver since that moment when two individuals first lived upon this earth, one has had what the other wanted, and has been willing for a consideration to part with his possession. This is the principle underlying all trade, however primitive, and all men, except the idlers, are merchants. ᘒᕦ

GREAT IS COMMERCE, AND
GREAT IS ITS FIELD OF WORK, OF
THOUGHT, OF DEVELOPMENT.

It is to the writer an almost incredible thing

that any Government could ever be so suicid-

ally short-sighted as to discourage trade; yet

history is full of the restrictions placed upon

it by the very men who would have profited

by making its path easier. ☙

The world is ripe for a new philosophy;
perhaps for a new religion, as understood
in its broadest meaning. We are hungry
for higher ideals, higher inspirations,
standards beyond those which man has
thus far conceived.

---

**WHEN THE GREEKS** reached their highest perfection in architecture, they had designed that which could not be surpassed. The proportions conceived by them remain in this twentieth century as the acknowledged standard of perfection: we cannot better their graceful lines. Man's character, however, is not governed by arithmetic but by imagination; and if our minds were not so extremely finite we should pierce through this wall of limitations and picture greater perfection, a higher type of man, a nobler ambition.

The world is ready for a great superhuman

mind which can break down the limits of

mental vision and give a new philosophy that

shall eliminate from the mind those little,

petty, mean elements which cause it to be

so earthy. ⚬❧

How rarely indeed are laws passed to encourage anything. They restrict, they limit, they prohibit from this and that; and as regards the man of Commerce their whole purpose seems to be too often to hamper and annoy.

The human animal is a most superb piece of machinery, and the mind is the most wonderful part of that machine; but man has allowed it to become clogged with old worn-out threads of prejudice, of hypocrisy, of cant, of inefficiency, of dullness, of snobbery, with the dust of a hundred undesirable things that mar the pattern of the fabric which this machine is trying to weave. ❧

*A* Brahmin prince, a thousand years before Christ, wrote a great epic poem, a poem of many volumes, and the striking thing in this wonderfully beautiful work is his description of the perfect character. We read his words three thousand years later and realize they describe our ideal. We have imagined nothing finer, nothing more nearly perfection. It is as if our idea of the best were a perfect circle which, as a circle, cannot be bettered.

OH, FOR A MENTAL GIANT WHO CAN BRUSH AWAY THIS WALL OF LIMITATIONS AND GIVE US NEW IDEAS OF LIFE!

DO BETTER OUR METHODS, OUR SYSTEMS.
THIS IS EASY BECAUSE THERE IS SO MUCH
LEFT TO ACCOMPLISH IN THAT DIRECTION
BEFORE PERFECTION IS REACHED, BUT OUR
MENTAL DEVELOPMENT IS LIMITED INDEED.

**JUST AS THE** foolish superstitious person surrounds himself with childish notions and distresses himself because he sees the moon over the wrong shoulder, or spills salt, or travels on a Friday—so in all phases and undertakings of life we are raising unnecessary obstacles which prevent our running the race well and swiftly. ॐ

WHY MUST ONE LEARN
TO THINK, AND WHY
CANNOT A PHILOSOPHY
BE CONCEIVED WHICH
MAKES THINKING AS
NATURAL AS SEEING?

One may feed a strong ox with a certain amount of undesirable food, and it will continue to be strong; but when that proportion is raised to a point beyond its ability to ignore, the animal suffers and finally dies. So a business may often seem to accept the false policy of its heads and still survive, but a poor policy cannot help in the upbuilding of a lasting fabric. ❧

**B**usiness does not always mean getting the better of someone else. Business does not stand for trickiness, for chicanery. Though business too often thrives when such practices are adopted, its thriving is in spite of these rather than by their aid. ❦

Honesty always pays. Honesty alone will never build a business, any more than good well-burnt bricks alone will build a house. But the policy of honesty, of scrupulous integrity, will, other things being reasonably equal, always win in the race for success. ❧

It is not clever to be too "shrewd." It is not good to get the better of another by hook or crook, by deception or falsehood. It is not only possible to be honest in business, but it is the height of unwisdom to be other than honest.

Exaggerated statements of any kind are dangerous, and no people are easier to compete against than those who use exaggeration. The world is not made up of fools, but of extremely worldly-wise people who recognize a knave with little difficulty. The trick is no longer the object of applause but of condemnation, and a trickster soon finds himself very much alone in business. ❧

*Why cannot business be conducted with the same sportsmanlike manliness as a game of football?*

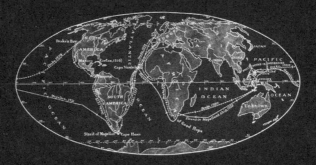

The newer philosophy of trade has been evolved and accepted by the leading men of business the world over. It has become their commercial Bible. They know that it brings the greatest success, but they know much more; they know it is putting, and in many communities has put, Commerce as a life work again into that splendid dignified position which it rightly held under the merchant-adventurers in the days of Queen Elizabeth. ॐ

AMBITION IS WONDERFULLY

VARIED, AND IT IS MOST

FORTUNATE THAT IT IS SO.

It is not Commerce which often makes the individual merchant narrow, mean, and dis-honest. It is the man himself who undignifies Commerce to the extent of his influence. ❧

*It is not the law which makes the little tricky, unscrupulous lawyer, it is the man himself, and it is generally he who makes men so hate that profession. It is the smallness of the man which makes us have disrespect for his calling; but with breadth of ideas, with nerve, with confidence in self, the man of Commerce can, and does, feel as proud of his sphere of action as can any man.*

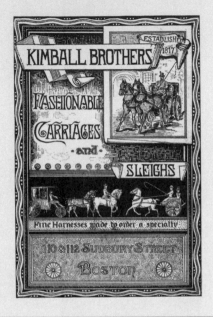

**TRADE IS THE** foundation of wealth. It is the great bedrock of strength upon which a nation is built. It should be nourished, cultivated, encouraged, appreciated, and praised. It should never be scorned. It is a magnificent servant which cannot be spoilt by kindness, but its enthusiasm can be checked, its virility weakened, its forcefulness taken away by indifference or worse. 🙰

ABILITY IS FINE, BUT ABILITY

ONLY BECOMES PRODUCTIVE

WITH PROPER TRAINING—A

TRAINING WHICH INCLUDES

ASSOCIATION WITH MEN STRONG

IN WILLPOWER AND GREAT IN

ACHIEVEMENT.

The man who first said, "Competition is the spice of life," uttered an aphorism which is indisputably true.

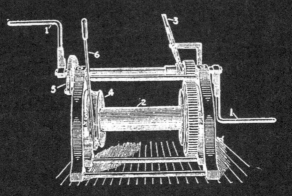

THE WORLD WANTS ANOTHER
FLOOD—A GREAT MENTAL
TORRENT TO WASH AWAY THE
ACCUMULATIONS OF FALSE IDEAS,
THE OBSTACLES, THE TRAPS,
WHICH TRIP AND HOLD FAST
AGAINST PROGRESS.

**THIS FACULTY OF** imagination is one of the most useful that the real man of Commerce can possess. It cuts the path through the forest of inexperience upon which judgment can more carefully walk. Imagination urges on. It is the yeast of progress. It pictures the desirable. It is like the architect's plan, while judgment and effort follow and build. No great thing was ever accomplished by the world's greatest men or greatest merchants without imagination. ❧

Go where you will, into the great cities or far afield to the out-of-the-way corners of the earth, there the thrifty Scot will be found trading and accumulating this world's goods. He is a hard man to bluff or to worst in an argument, and a competitor who is never wisely ignored.

We of this age have been given tools with which to work and accomplish of which our merchant forefathers never dreamed. Machinery—steam—electricity, have made one day's work equal to ten or a hundred, and the experience of all of our predecessors is ours if we choose to take it. ॐ

Man's mind is finite, but it should be no more limited now than five hundred or two thousand years ago. If, then, we enter the lists with the same virility, determination, nerve, and imagination, it would seem that the twentieth-century man of commerce should far surpass the merchants of Phoenicia, Venice, or Augsburg.

The day of physical adventure is over. The day of the bold Phoenician, the fearless trader who with his caravan threaded his way into unknown lands; the day when the early English merchant-sailor trusted and risked his fortune in one small boat, and sought out markets and trading points in undiscovered corners of the earth—these days are gone forever. The earth has all been "discovered," its lands and peoples are known, and its oceans charted. ❧

*The world is smaller. Steam and electricity, great ships, railways, and many recorded experiences have made it so; but as the circumference of this earth has seemed to diminish, its commercial undertakings have grown greater.*

The man of business of the twentieth century differs enormously from the merchant-adventurer of the fourteenth, fifteenth, and sixteenth centuries in his methods and the tools with which he works. The last hundred years have shown him that one man cannot do it all, and that anyone who attempts to hold within his two hands all the threads of a great business of the present day fails to achieve the greatest success.

Is it not surprising how, throughout history, the chief occupation of all rulers of all nations has been to get money? If this money, all these uncountable sums of money collected or wrung from the people, had been used intelligently or even with reasonable good sense, what wonders could have been accomplished. ॐ

The great Distributing House or Department Store, so called for the want of a better title, may be permitted to represent the modern spirit of organization. It is to the writer the most interesting of all forms of business, and by its constant and necessary publicity it occupies perhaps the most conspicuous place in the public mind. It usually employs the greatest number of people, and must seek employees of the higher grade of intelligence. It frequently, therefore, pays out in salaries and wages a larger sum weekly than any other single business, and is more often approached by those seeking opportunity to work than any other. Its daily transactions are large in volume, its cash handled is very great. It is intimately associated with every family in the community in supplying them with the necessities of life, and thus by force of circumstances enters into the daily life of the city in which it is. ❧

Men of genius and wonderful nerve and determination, who in the Dark Ages would have been conquering princes, have in these later years thrown their ability into Commerce and have conquered, not territory and slaves, but trade and its child, money, from any and every part of the world where trade was to be found. ❧

The merchant sends the buyer far afield with instructions to invest a greater or less sum of money in such goods, either staples or novelties, as he thinks will interest the home public. He risks his money and a certain amount of prestige upon the judgment of the buyer, to whom an intimate knowledge of the public's wishes and whims, and of the department's ability to sell profitably what he buys, is absolutely necessary to remove as much as possible of the element of risk. Much merchandise begins to depreciate from the day it arrives; practically none increases in value. The buyer then must learn to buy enough and not too much; to buy what will give satisfaction when sold again; to pay not too much for what he buys; to know qualities and values; to spend his employer's money wisely and well.

There are enough mistakes made and poor judgment shown, as we all know, in that field of activity called Commerce; but if one-tenth of the foolishness had been employed there that has been exhibited by those who have undertaken to govern, all commerce, and everyone connected with it, would have been bankrupt many times over and have sunk long since in the seas of oblivion. ❧

A GREAT DEPARTMENT STORE

MUST ALWAYS DEPEND VITALLY

UPON ITS STAFF.

The process of warp and woof entered slowly but surely into the very lives of the people, for just as certain trees and plants are indigenous to certain countries and districts, so certain departments of commerce seem to belong to certain races of people. Their children and their children's children saw the work being done as soon as their eyes were open, until it became as natural for a child of the north to weave cloth as it is for a child of Italy to sing, or of Iceland to fish.

**YET ENGLAND CAN,** if she will, again become by far the greatest manufacturing center of the world. She can, if she will, snap her fingers at competition. She does it admirably in some branches of trade, why not in all? 🙠

THE SUPERVISORS OF
MERCHANDISE, OR MERCHANDISE
MANAGERS, MUST BE STUDENTS
OF MEN, OF MARKETS,
OF THE SCIENCE OF TRADING,
AND OF FIGURES.

To the merchandise manager a detailed report in figures is as clear and as enlightening as the compass to the navigator. It tells him how his ship of trade is going. It keeps him away from rocks and shoals, and shows where the water is open and clear. ❧

The merchandise managers must cultivate conservative judgment and must be free from impulsive hysteria. Conservatism does not mean always saying "no," but may be defined as a careful forethought, ready to endorse risk when risk can be afforded, and when accompanied with the chance of probable success. The merchant is not a speculator beyond the necessities of his business. Its exigencies require a certain gamble, but one in which the purely speculative is eliminated as far as human ability and thoughtful experience can contrive. The merchant's province is to buy or produce and sell. It is not within his sphere of activity to sell what he has not, nor to "corner" any product, nor to trade beyond his financial or commercial abilities. ✌

Men and women become infatuated with an idea, and so bereft of usual financial judgment that their acts when viewed from a distance appear insane, as indeed they often really are.

To be conservative means to be wisely careful, more ready to say "yes" than "no" but only ready with "yes" when a clear road ahead is evident; optimistic and enthusiastic on principle, but keenly alive to possible pitfalls; determined to do, to work, to think, to accomplish, but with eyes wide open, and hand always on the steering wheel. ❧

Or to be conservative may mean to let well enough alone; to adopt as one's motto, "What was good enough for my grandfather is good enough for me;" to say "no" always, because it is easier and requires less effort to let things rest as they are rather than give one's sanction to a change, a possible advance. To shrink from the responsibility of trying anything which has not already been tried. In short, such conservatism means standing still rather than advancing. It is the opposite of progress. It is the result of mental laziness and physical inactivity. It hates imagination, shuns progress, fears anything new, and guided by this kind of conservatism no nation-State, business, or individual has done great things or left a creditable impress on the period in which it or he lived. &

**TO THE MAN** whose mind is active, fads are a delightful rest, and the busier the man, the more desirable are hobbies to which he can turn. Healthy fads are heartily to be commended, but fads carried to too great an extreme too often lead to sorrow. 🙶

The time has passed when an irritable customer, no matter who he or she may be, can, whether right or wrong, ride rough-shod over the young man or woman behind the counter and demand his or her dismissal, and it is a good thing it is so. There are always two sides to every question, and even when mistakes are made they are usually of the head and not the heart, and the precept to be laid down by the staff manager to employees should be, "Don't make the same mistake twice." He is often sitting as a judge, upon whose decision depends the success or failure of the young man or woman who may be just starting out in life. Fairness is, therefore, a prime quality. ⚘

To the wise managers of men encouragement more often than fault-finding brings the better service and loyalty, and anyone who has ever served in a minor capacity knows that a well-earned "pat on the back" will make the blood flow faster and do more to cement the loyalty and determination to do continually better than any number of scantily earned reprimands. The managers of staff must, therefore, find it as easy to say a pleasant thing as to reprove, and must know when to administer praise or blame. ❧

This ability, therefore, to organize, to breathe into others that fire of enthusiasm, that quality of judgment, that spirit of progress, has long been considered by thinking men of commerce as the final and greatest of all qualities, the test of supreme commercial genius. ❧

It WOULD BE ENORMOUSLY INTERESTING COULD WE GET INTO COMMUNICATION WITH MARS OR SOME INHABITED PLANET OTHER THAN OUR OWN AND LEARN HOW ITS PEOPLE ARE DOING THINGS. SUPPOSE STEAM AND ITS POWER HAD NEVER BEEN DISCOVERED, HOW DIFFERENT OUR LIVES WOULD BE. SUPPOSE THE WEAVING OF FIBERS, OR MOLDING OF IRON, OR THE USE OF ELECTRICITY, OR THE DISCOVERY OF PRINTING, OR THE MAKING OF PAPER HAD NEVER COME ABOUT.

The selling of merchandise is the primary reason for existence of a distributing business. Something new, something better must constantly be thought of, and the imagination of the sales manager must devise continually fresh schemes for the stimulus of sales.

[THE SALES MANAGER] MUST PUT HIMSELF
IN THE PLACE OF THE PUBLIC. HE MUST
THINK FROM THE STANDPOINT OF THE
CUSTOMER. HE MUST DREAM OUT THE
IDEAL, ALLOWING HIS THOUGHTS TO
RUN WILD, AND THEN BY BRINGING
JUDGMENT AND EXPERIENCE TO HIS AID
AND DISCARDING THE IMPRACTICAL AND
USELESS, CRYSTALLIZE THE THOUGHT INTO
WORKABLENESS. NEITHER MUST HE EXPECT
NOR ATTEMPT TO DO ALL THE THINKING
OR IMAGINING HIMSELF, BUT MUST BE
QUICK TO RECEIVE AND ACT ON THE
SUGGESTIONS OF OTHERS, ALWAYS GIVING
THEM FULL CREDIT FOR WHAT THEY HAVE
PROPOSED.

If one cannot learn from others, one can only be interested in comparisons when they are in one's own favor, and such a policy is only comparable with that of the ostrich whose head is buried in the sand, again demonstrating how necessary is the open mind. ❧

THE GOLDEN RULE OF TREATING
OTHERS AS ONE WOULD LIKE
TO BE TREATED IS AS WISE AND
PRACTICAL IN THE BUSINESS OF
MANAGING A STAFF AS IT WAS IN
THE SERMON ON THE MOUNT,
AND HAS IN THIS TWENTIETH
CENTURY BEEN ADOPTED AS
A GUIDING PRINCIPLE BY THE
MOST EMINENTLY SUCCESSFUL
MANAGERS OF MEN.

Every division of a great department store

is fascinating to one whose mind grasps and

enjoys details, and this faculty is an absolute

essential to the managers of selling. ⁊❧

As necessity is the mother of invention, so it and imagination are the two parents of originality, which is a prime necessity in a business already surpassing in development and excellence in its almost infinite details and ramifications any previous business in the world's history.

Originality of one kind is appallingly rare; such originality as produces an absolutely new idea, which reaches out into the blue sky and grasps a thought that has not been known before, and as the world of civilization grows older it becomes increasingly difficult to do so.

BUT THE KIND OF SEEMING ORIGINALITY WHICH IS MORE OFTEN USED CONSISTS OF ADAPTING AN OLD IDEA TO A NEW BRANCH OF ACTIVITY. FOR EXAMPLE, THE KNITTING-MACHINE AT FIRST WAS BUT THE ADAPTATION TO MACHINERY OF THE MOVEMENTS OF THE FINGERS OF THE HAND-KNITTER. IT WAS MARVELOUSLY INGENIOUS, BUT IT WAS NEVERTHELESS ADAPTATION. THE AIRPLANE IS BUT THE SUSTAINING POWER OF GREAT STIFF WINGS, AS WE CONSTANTLY SEE USED BY THE SEAGULL WHEN FLYING AGAINST THE WIND, COUPLED WITH THE INTERNAL EXPLOSION ENGINE WHICH HAS BEEN IN USE FOR YEARS.

Progressive conservatism—if we may use this term—takes progress to its arms; it feels that nothing is "good enough" which can be better, that our grandfathers' methods and results should, wherever possible, be surpassed. It stands for effort, no matter at what physical or mental cost, if that effort will place the foot a step further toward what may be called better. Such conservatism is optimistic, happy, and never tiring, but it brackets all effort with the principle of intelligent forethought.

SELF-CONTENTMENT FINDS NO CHAIR,
NO PLACE FOR REPOSE IN THE MODERN
BUSINESS WHICH HAS FOR ITS MOTTO
"EXCELSIOR."

The figures of a business are like

the log of a ship. They show just where

the business is, how fast it is going,

how far it is from port, how its supplies

are holding out.

The fact is, many people are going through their daily duties too much because they think they must, rather than because they love to, but the man who approaches business with a joy in the work becomes a very much more difficult competitor than one who does his work because he has to and flees from it the first moment he can. ❧

THE CHIEF REQUIREMENTS
FOR MANAGERSHIP ARE
JUDGMENT, PROMPTNESS
OF ACTION AS OPPOSED
TO PROCRASTINATION,
TACT, AND A
MATHEMATICAL MIND.

The supervisor simply watches percentages, increase and decrease, and advises those who spend of the result of his figures. He is a sort of daily historian, a weather gauge, who records results for the benefit of those responsible. He is at the back of the firing line. His eyes are on the figures, and whatever credit he gets in no way detracts from the credit due to the other man. ❧

on the character of the house, and his
ambitious breadth of view, knowledge
of the world, and good judgment will,
when competition is strong and healthy,
determine the results of his house.

Business success is by no means the only aim in life, but with the real merchant it is one of the aims, and one that employs a large number of hours in every day and week. ❧

*The head of the business must know at least in a general way the daily duties and the requirements of each of his lieutenants, though he need not necessarily be a master in each of the varied branches of effort.*

**O**pportunity is what the quick-thinking, energetic man most looks for in this world. ❧

What is success? Pedagogically "the favorable attainment of anything attempted," but what then is the thing to attempt? The work of life!

We may say that we believe that Success
in its broadest meaning is the favorable
attainment of that object or series
of objects which makes for a higher
standard of civilization, which gives to
the world higher ideals in those things,
which concern the everyday life of the
multitude.

The people count for more than ever before in the world's history. The so-called common people, the multitude, make themselves continually more felt. They control more, and their power grows with every added year; and that man who by word or speech or example or works causes the great body of plain people to think on higher planes, to strive after a finer quality of living, who causes the brain of the people to throb faster and on more nearly perfect lines, that man lifts humanity into a higher realm, enlarges its horizon, makes men happier, broader-minded, more self-respecting, and more dignified, and the degree with which he does this shall define the degree of his Success. ❧

**OPPORTUNITY IS THE** road—sometimes broad and smooth, often rough and difficult—but always the road along which one may tread toward that goal called Success. ❧

It is his to do as he will, and the quality of his doing is determined by the height of his ideals and his strength of purpose. Inactivity—doing nothing—simply enjoying himself, while perhaps agreeable, does not and cannot in this twentieth century stand for the highest success.

For as truly as the captain of the ship decides before weighing anchor for which port he is to sail, and as he proceeds in his voyage carefully plans out the following day's duties, so every man, every State, every nation should, if possessing sufficient moral courage and ability, decide, "What is the thing to be accomplished? What is the goal? What is the man, the State, the nation here for?"

Work, good, hard, honest work, will achieve almost any material thing in this world, and work may be delightful, noble, exhilarating, fascinating. Work may be full of excitement, of satisfaction, of joy and happiness. ❧

OF ALL GOLDEN CHANCES, OF
ALL DEPARTMENTS OF ENDEAVOR,
NONE, NONE PRESENTS SUCH
INFINITE AND KALEIDOSCOPIC,
ALWAYS CHANGING
OPPORTUNITIES AS DOES THAT
BROADEST, SUREST FIELD OF
EFFORT CALLED COMMERCE.

For people's ideas of many things, including morals, change as the centuries go by. We hold up our hands and make round rings of our mouths at the bare thought of such an annoying custom as systematic wrecking, yet many of our own most ordinary proceedings will probably be considered as highly immoral by the people of A.D. 2500.

**ALL MEN ARE** made of the same clay, and all, more or less, in time seem to be influenced by the same passions and desires. In those old days kings and people in high authority, with increased power, grew more and more autocratic, and to these wonderful old merchants came, with a greater ability to have their unimpeded way, an inclination to override any who opposed their wishes.

If society frowns upon all work, or effort,

except that connected with the Army or

Navy or perhaps some governmental post,

then unfortunately for the country the young

men—members of the so-called governing

class—will flock into these occupations and

let the others suffer. ໃ

There is in every country a limit to the number who can be satisfactorily employed permanently as officers in the Army or Navy, as diplomats, or as members of the working staff of the Government. These positions, it is needless to say, must be filled with intelligent men, but equal encouragement should be given to those in other spheres of influence.

Not all the people of a country seek after the same thing—not to all do the charms of winning appeal. To some men Commerce, the science of making, of buying and selling, seems uninviting, and some are still foolish enough to think it undignified and mean. 

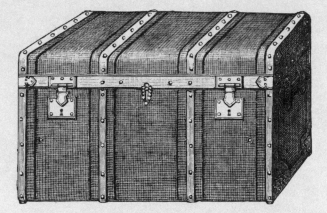

Let us take as an example the question of advertisement. We need a new philosophy here. Why should a statement be subject to question? Is it not infinitely wiser to make every statement dependable beyond the chance of question? Why pay for space and then fill it with matter which must quickly be discovered to be false? Why thus reduce the value of every future statement? And yet this is exactly what is continually being done in many parts of the world.

Pettiness is being dethroned from the place in trade to which it never had a right, and big, broad, sportsmanlike ideas have taken its place. That one must consider a competitor as necessarily other than a friend has gone with all the other discarded beliefs. It is no more true of business than of cricket or baseball.

It is wise to be very liberal with the public, and to give something which could be charged for is no longer a business error but quite the reverse. It is desperately silly to hold wages down to the breaking point; for there is so much more to the employee than two arms and two legs. There is the spirit of enthusiasm and earnestness and "I will," which means more to the employer than ten pairs of arms and legs.

AND LOYALTY IS A QUALITY TO

BE EARNED BY THE EMPLOYER

FROM THE EMPLOYEE, AND ONLY

EARNED BY FAIR, FRIENDLY,

GENEROUS TREATMENT.

᙮

**BUT TRADE, WITH** its broader, safer road to financial success, is coming into its own. The old must give way to the new, and the philosophy of the leaders in the world's Commerce is diametrically opposed to all those old unprincipled principles. ❧

Men who have adopted Commerce as their medium of activity are working on the played-out philosophy of trade which sprang up after the sturdy old merchant-adventurers ceased to exist; that false philosophy which thought it was clever to be too shrewd; that it was good business always to try to get the better of the other; that it was impossible to be honest in business; that exaggeration, spoken or written, was not only necessary but clever; that nearly everyone was a fool, and fools could best be handled by knaves; that a trick which meant a cheat was something to applaud; that nothing must be given which could be charged for; that no one must be paid more than could be helped; that the stronger was quite right in oppressing the weak; that might was always right when dealing with employees; that loyalty, if desirable, was to be obtained through fear rather than through justice or affection; that competition involved personal antagonism; that a large outlay or production was usually foolish, and that hoarding was the only way to wealth; and so on until one is nauseated with the littlenesses which crowded out the broader philosophy. ❧

THE MEN WHOSE MOTTO WAS
"NOTHING VENTURE NOTHING
HAVE" WERE SURELY MORE
LIKELY TO ACCOMPLISH REALLY
GREAT THINGS THAN THE MERE
PLODDERS BY PENURIOUS SAVING.

❧

Personally, I should like to see a revival of the fine old spirit of the merchant-adventurers. Broad commerce still offers an opportunity to the flower of England's young men, but too many are blind to her outstretched arms.

*A great business may, in a way, become almost a principality, and under broad, capable administration make princes of its members—merchant princes.*

Just as life is often so much of a gamble, so the making of a fortune possesses almost always in its formula a large quantity of risk. This is not the risk of the lottery kind, which brings success or failure on the turn of the card, nor does it depend on the element of pure chance which so many call luck. But it stakes its future on the judgment of its leader; it bets on its own conclusions. ❧

The absolutely sure things in this world
are not so interesting, to say the least of it,
as those which may not win, but which in
winning win big stakes. Anything which
places a barrier against progress, against
walking in any but the old frequently trod-
den paths, tends to dry up the springs of
imagination. ❧

*The head of a great business house must be a really capable man; otherwise its prestige weakens, and competitors who are everywhere wrest its position from it. But herein lies much of the fascination of a business career.*

Broad Commerce is the best school. It gives men confidence in themselves without self-satisfaction or conceit. It develops the imagination and encourages high ideals; it teaches them to think and to work with their whole might.

A life spent in Commerce may, to many, seem full of drudgery, but so may be the life given to discovery, to invention, to art, to the study and practice of the law, to diplomacy and politics, or to any other undertaking. It is indeed not unreasonable to argue that there are fewer hours of tiresome, tedious, uninteresting labor spent in Commerce than in any other serious pursuit. ❧

The old kings, from whom the society of the day was wont to take its cue, were in many cases wise enough to encourage Commerce to their utmost, and found it to their advantage to do so. And in our own day we see some great leaders giving every encouragement to Commerce.

It is within the power of Society to insist upon dignity in Commerce, and withhold her approval from the pettiness which is found on the lower fringe of trading; but she surely errs if she casts a disdainful eye on the whole industry, and allows such snobbishness to become in any way fashionable.

YOUNG MEN WHOSE POSITION
MAKES THEM INDEPENDENT
ARE GREATLY INFLUENCED BY
THE ATTITUDE OF THOSE WITH
WHOM THEY ARE THROWN,
AS TO THE BUSINESS OR
PROFESSION INTO WHICH THEY
ARE TO PLACE THEMSELVES.

&

Commerce, broad not narrow, bold not timid,

liberal not mean, energetic not lazy, can be as

dignified as any other calling or profession.

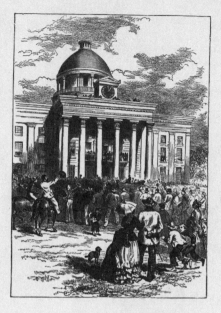

Adam Smith wrote one hundred

and fifty years ago: "All original

wealth comes from the soil."

SYSTEM IS ALWAYS THE SERVANT,
NEVER THE MASTER, AND
FURTHERMORE A SERVANT WHICH
IMPROVES WITH EACH ADDED
SEASON'S PRACTICE, AND IT IS
THE PLEASURABLE TASK OF THE
MANAGERS OF THE SYSTEMS OF
THE HOUSE TO SEE THAT THE
SYSTEMS ARE ALWAYS MODERN AND
THE BEST THAT CAN BE DEVISED.

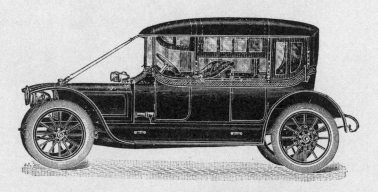

**THE MAN POSSESSING** many lands, he especially would be a merchant in fact, and sell, but his is a merchandise which too often nowadays waits in vain for the buyer.

In a large house, secondary only to its published matter are the displays of merchandise. This too is a kind of advertising. The dressing out of the departments and the windows is done by highly specialized artists, men who study a window with the same care that the stage manager or scenic artist studies his stage effects. Window displays are designed, constructed, and actually dressed in the studios before they are placed in the windows. They often require months of study and months for execution. It is an art, and a very costly art, but it is worth all that it costs. 🐦

System is the servant which keeps the machinery straight. It is here, there, everywhere. It must never make itself felt except through its beneficial results. It must be known by its works. System which is obtrusive is irritating; it becomes red-tapism. System is like gravity; it acts without being apparent. In a great organization it is an imperative necessity, but wisdom in management quickly cuts off any piece of so-called system which has failed to justify its existence. ॐ

Graceful palms are as much a part of a comprehensive store scheme as are other decorations, and in fact the whole world of color and of art are considered by the artistic window-dresser as his field of supply.

*As* all parts of a business are worked on a mathematical system, the manager of sales must be an adept at figures, to whom a table of comparative percentages is as clear as the primer. He must, therefore, be highly practical as well as imaginative.

PRECEDENT SHOULD
HAVE LITTLE PLACE IN
A PROGRESSIVE BUSINESS, A
PROGRESSIVE GOVERNMENT,
OR A PROGRESSIVE NATION.

To act always according to precedent is to acknowledge that one's ability to think and judge is inferior to that of one's grandfathers, and to assume with a blind stupidity that nothing is right which has not been accepted long ago. Steps had to be taken once: they were taken, and as often as not proved to be errors of judgment. No matter, the steps were taken, and right or wrong they are the only ones to be taken again. ∂

HOW EXTRAORDINARY IT IS
THAT MEN CAN BE FOUND WHO,
FAILING IN NERVE OR BRAIN
POWER, FOLLOW LIKE BLINDED
SHEEP SOME FALSE LEADER OF A
CENTURY AGO SIMPLY BECAUSE HE
DID LIVE A CENTURY AGO.

*It is fortunate for the empire that few of the younger men accept the theory that whatever was is right, and generally prefer to think for themselves, while those who stick to many of the old worn-out, moth-eaten policies of the Mid-Victorian era must by the laws of nature before very long retire from the direction of this world's affairs and seek final rest somewhere where things never change.*

*System is like oil, but it is much more than this. It not only keeps the machinery cool and free from friction, but it is almost the machinery itself. System, according to the modern department stores' acceptation of the word, means "the best way to do things."*

**GOOD JUDGMENT OF** course is the foundation stone upon which the whole fabric rests. Good judgment should, if possible, permeate the entire organization from top to bottom. A faulty decision, an error of judgment, is expensive, not necessarily in money only but also in prestige. ❧

About half a century ago, a few shopkeepers became inoculated with the spirit of enterprise. They grew beyond the little shop by the simple process of addition and came to recognize the building which was the house of the expanding business as something of importance to be thought of and be made better. Then it was that department stores in their early stages began to appear and from then until now they have continued to develop in every direction, and no man can foresee their final form and size, or say where they will stop. ❧

# ABOUT THE AUTHOR

*H*arry Gordon Selfridge (1856–1947) was born in Ripon, Wisconsin. His family later moved to Michigan, where his father ran a store until the outbreak of the Civil War. Selfridge began work at ten years old, delivering newspapers. At twenty he took a job at the Chicago store run by Marshall Field. In 1890, he married Rose Buckingham, by whom he had four children.

In 1906, on holiday in London, Selfridge determined to start a department store in the city, run on American lines. Three years later he founded Selfridges on Oxford Street, which was founded on the principles enumerated in this book. He remained with the store until 1941, though he lost a great deal of his fortune in the Depression. By the time he retired from business, he had squandered much of his money on a lavish lifestyle and a series of love affairs after the death of his wife in 1918. He died in London and is buried next to his wife in Dorset.